POSH PROTOCOL Volume 1

~

The

10 Commandments *of*

Christian Accouterment For Women

POSH PROTOCOL Volume 1

~

The

10 Commandments *of*

Christian Accouterment For Women

C. C. Preston • Dr. Posh ®

Copyright © 2017

Copyright © 2017 C.C. Preston, Dr. Posh® All rights reserved. Author Photos Purchased. Printed in the United States. No part of this book may be used or reproduced in any form or manner without written permission, except in the case of brief quotations embodied in articles and reviews.

ISBN 10: 0-692-87560-3
ISBN 13: 978-0-692-87560-5

TO

Imar, O'Bryan & Uziah

Skyler, Dennis & Zion

CONTENTS

POSH PROTOCOL
Defined   1

POSH PROTOCOL
Awards and Faux Pas   5

Thou Shall Have No
Hair Rollers [Or Sleeping Bonnets]
On Thy Head In Public Areas   11

Thou Shall Not
Neglect Thy Skin
[Or Conceal Such Neglect
With Make-Up]   15

Thou Shall Not
Expose Thy Cleavage
[Or Intimate Parts Of Thy Body]
In Public Areas   19

Remember
Thou Does Not Have A Cloak Of
Invisibility &
Thou Always Has An Audience   23

CONTENTS

Honor God
With Thy Whole Body
At All Times   27

Thou Shall Not
Expose Thy Undergarments
In Public Areas   31

Thou Shall Not
Don Inappropriate
Eye-Steering Apparel   35

Thou Shall Not
Don Accessories Bearing
Ungodly Symbols or Insignia   39

Thou Shall Not
Don Pajamas or Robes
[Or Other Private Quarters Garments]
In Public Areas   43

Thou Shall Not
Omit [Full-Length Mirror]
Wardrobe Checks   47

ACKNOWLEDGMENTS

Giving Honor and Thanks to my
Lord and Savior Jesus Christ.
I am nothing without God.

Posh Protocol Prayer

Father God,
May we always embrace elegant etiquette in speech, adornment, actions and deeds. Father God, allow our manner of being to always be a pleasant, polished and posh *reflection of You and Your Kingdom.*

In the Name of Jesus, Amen

*"Let all things be done decently and in order"
(1 Corinthians 14:40, King James Version)*

POSH PROTOCOL

Defined

The term Posh is synonymous with luxury, elegance and opulence. [1] Protocol is defined as "the customs and regulations dealing with diplomatic formality, precedence, and etiquette."[2] Posh Protocol™ is elegant etiquette in speech, adornment, actions or deeds.

Posh Protocol™ is a representation of the regality of the Kingdom of God. Posh Protocol™ is a reflection of the elegant workings of the Kingdom of God. God has a standard of excellence for our way of being, our way of thinking and our way of living.

The manifestation of our individual personal Posh Protocol™ is the result of a deep internal desire within each of us to embrace and exhibit elegant etiquette in speech, adornment, actions or deeds. Mastery of our Posh Protocol™ requires receiving the instructions of the Holy Spirit, as well as, discipline, diligence and dedication.

God reminds us of the stewardship he has granted unto us as overseers over our own lives in Titus 1. Therefore we are not to be "arrogant or quick-tempered or a drunkard or violent or greedy for gain" but on the contrary we are to be "hospitable, a lover of good, self-controlled, upright, holy, and disciplined" (Titus 1:7-8). This scriptural reference instructs us to activate and embrace our inner Posh Protocol™.

As heirs to Gods Kingdom, royalty is our inheritance. Elegance is our daily manifestation and opulence envelops our eternal destination. Gods will for our lives, will be done. This is made perfectly clear in Isaiah 55:11 where Gods thunderous voice states "So shall my word be that goeth forth out of my mouth: it shall not return unto me void, but is shall accomplish that which I please, and it shall prosper in the thing whereto I sent it." Yes and Amen

Posh Protocol Awards And Faux Pas

The **Posh Protocol Diamond Award**™ is an award bestowed for elegant etiquette in speech, adornment, actions or deeds. The recipient (s) receiving such an award may receive verbal or electronic notification informing him/her of the award. The Posh Protocol Diamond Award may be **awarded multiple times** throughout the calendar year.

The **Posh Protocol Politesse Award**™ is our highest award bestowed for distinguished, elegant etiquette in speech, adornment, actions or deeds. The recipient receiving such an award may receive verbal or electronic notification informing him/her of the award.

The Posh Protocol Politesse Award is **awarded once annually** to an individual or organization that has been chosen from among all award nominees during the preceding calendar year.

A **Posh Protocol Faux Pas**™ is an error in formality or etiquette, in speech, adornment, actions or deeds. The person(s) committing such an error may receive verbal or electronic notification informing him/her that such an error has occurred based on evidence witnessed, documented and reported. A Posh Protocol Faux Pas may be **dispensed multiple times** throughout the calendar year.

A **Posh Protocol *Verbal* Faux Pas**™ may include words, sayings or sentence structure that are indecent, uncouth, rude, vulgar, etc. (The Verbal No Fly List includes profanity, derogatory slang and other word weapons.)

A **Posh Protocol *Wardrobe* Faux Pas**™ may include apparel, accessories or footwear that are indecorous in form (style, length, color, etc.) and/or function (fit, cut, etc.) or used for a purpose for which they were not intended.

The 10 Commandments Of Christian Accouterment For Women

Thou Shall Have No Hair Rollers [Or Sleeping Bonnets] On Thy Head In Public Areas

Please Stop It! I understand that you would like to preserve your coiffure until the time of its proper unveiling. However, unless you are staying within private quarters the rollers and bonnets must depart from your head and enter their proper storage containers. No exceptions. Even if you have booked a seat on a red-eye and are scheduled to attend a wedding at first light, you are still not exempt from this commandment.

Please use Godly judgment when deciding what hairstyle, cut and color to wear daily and for special occasions. Remember to give your hairline the attention it deserves. Refrain from hairstyles that put undue stress and tension on your hairline. Always display hair that is clean and neat. Technology and culture continues to expand quite rapidly, regarding hair color, hairstyles, lengths and textures. It is refreshing that so many hair options are now available.

Hair Extensions as a hair styling option have become increasingly prevalent in our culture. Quality and texture varies greatly with hair extensions. Take some time to research the type, texture and brand of hair extensions that are needed for the style you are trying to achieve. Hair extensions that are 100% human hair will provide a more authentic replication of your own natural hair.

Quality hair extensions may last through several installations over a one or two year period. Your undercarriage, your natural hair underneath your hair extensions, will still need to be cared for, including a hair protecting moisturizer, such as a leave-in liquid conditioner.

Perucas (wigs) have also risen in popularity and use. When choosing a peruca, inspect the construction of its base. A well designed and well constructed peruca base, will be instrumental in its longevity

Thou Shall Not Neglect Thy Skin [Or Conceal Such Neglect With Make-Up]

Skin is the largest human organ. Beautiful skin is clean healthy skin. Step One, Cleanse. Cleanse your facial skin using a washcloth or an electric face brush. Refrain from using only your hands with soap, to cleanse your face. Human hands are most often teeming with bacteria. One crucial way in which to keep our skin clean is to keep our hands off of it.

Do not rest your hands on your face or on any other part of your skin. Clean objects or surfaces regularly that come in contact with your skin, such as door knobs, car steering wheels, cell phones, etc. Step Two, Moisturize. Select a moisturizer formulated for your skin type that is infused with sunscreen. Yes, even oily skin requires a (oil-free) moisturizer.

Adequate nutrition, hydration, and exercise also play a crucial role in achieving and maintaining healthy skin. Make it your goal to have healthy glowing skin prior to applying makeup.

Now that your skin is clean and healthy, it is time to select some quality cosmetics, if you so choose. Step Three, Apply Cosmetics. The powerhouse components of cosmetic application are foundation, eyebrow sculpting and cheek color. Start by choosing the correct shade(s) of foundation and concealer. Plan on using more than one shade of each, given the seasonal changes in skin tone and the need for contouring. Color choices for eyes, cheeks and lips should compliment your skin tone and skin type.

    Do not underestimate the power of the eyebrow. Invest in an eyebrow stencil if your freestyle fill-in technique has not been perfected. A variety of gels, powders and pencils are available for eyebrow sculpting. For a professionally polished make-up look, bespeak a professional make-up artist (MUA) to apply your make-up with expert precision.

Thou Shall Not Expose Thy Cleavage [Or Intimate Parts Of Thy Body] In Public Areas

Welcome to the No Cleavage Zone! Garment Closure, No Exposure! Close your clothes. God instructs us in Ephesians 6:14-17, to put on spiritual armor, "the breastplate of righteousness" and the "helmet of salvation" likewise, physically covering our intimate body parts while in public areas, is for our own protection from the exploitive devices of the enemy.

Low cut blouses and high cut skirts are conveying a message that may serve as an advertisement for ungodly activity. Your worth is not based on your physical attributes. Your value is far above rubies (Proverbs 31:10). Do not forget your Godly status when choosing garments to wear and how to wear them. Make the right decision to cover your cleavage and other intimate parts of your body while in public areas. You have been made the righteousness of God through Christ Jesus. Remember who you are and whose you are. Amen

Don Your Diadem™ (put on your crown) and stand tall. Walk in and take your rightful place in the Kingdom of God, a place of holy inheritance. Our royal inheritance is decreed in 1 Peter 2:9 which states, "But ye are a chosen generation, a royal priesthood, an holy nation, a peculiar people; that ye should show forth the praises of him who hath called you out of darkness into his marvelous light:"

The time is now to permanently shift your wardrobe behavior by internally renouncing any inappropriate attention seeking desires along with any insatiable desires for admiration from others. God sees us. It is his desire that we crave his attention. The word of God tells us to "delight thyself also in the Lord; and he shall give thee the desires of thine heart. Commit thy way unto the Lord; trust also in him;...." (Psalm 37:4-5).

Remember
Thou Does Not Have
A Cloak
Of Invisibility &
Thou Always Has
An Audience

Yes, we can see you! You are not invisible. No, we are not staring at you because you are 'stop and stare' gorgeous, while that may be true, we are staring at you, due to our astonishment of what you are wearing or the lack thereof.

In our current societal whirlwind of super speed and micro sized technology, we *always* have an audience. Our planet hosts a population of over seven billion people. So it is important to remember, our environment *is* our audience. Our environment is teeming with cameras of all types from all heights and directions that are keeping a watchful on us. More importantly, those closest to us, our family, friends and fellow Christians are watching us.

We are continually conversing with our audience before ever speaking a word. Let us ensure that our unspoken message is one of self-respect and reverence unto God.

Most importantly, God is all seeing and all knowing. He is constantly observing his children. "Can any hide himself in secret places that I shall not see him? saith the Lord. Do not I fill heaven and earth? saith the Lord" (Jeremiah 23:24). There is nowhere we can go and nowhere we can hide where God himself will not find us and explore our hearts. It is futile to attempt to shield your heart against the watchful eye of God. It is his desire that we live our lives according to our divine destiny revealed to us in his word.

Remembering we always have an audience helps to establish the importance of our perpetual Godly representation. The Holy Spirit is a ceaseless source of help in times of uncertainty. Always pray and ask for guidance. Always refer to the Holy Bible, the only infallible instruction manual for life.

Honor God With Thy Whole Body At All Times

Do not deface or dishonor the magnificence of your own body. You are not your own, "for ye are bought with a price: therefore glorify God in your body, and in your spirit, which are God's" (1 Corinthians 6:20). God dwells within each of us, thusly it should forever be our desire to present our body as a holy dwelling place unto the Lord. Honoring God with our whole body is the also the highest form of honoring ourselves.

Our human body does have frailties, which require daily care and daily maintenance. In addition, an annual health maintenance schedule is needed. This schedule should include, a physical exam, bi-annual teeth cleanings, etc. Meditation on the word of God, maintaining a well balanced diet, and engaging in physical exercise is essential as well. Health and wellness should be a top priority, "for in him we live and move, and have our being; . . ." (Acts 17:28).

Consider your decision very carefully when contemplating *elective* permanent changes to your body. Tattoos, body piercings, and body carvings are often irreversible. These types of body modifications are sometimes desired during a specific time period in ones life, as an act of personal expression. Commemoration of a special occasion may also prompt permanent body modification. In Leviticus 19:28, God addresses this topic for us, to assist us in self-preservation.

Permanent body modification in the form of cosmetic surgery seems to have gained popularity in recent years. These surgical procedures are no longer as cost prohibitive as they were in the past. While the costs of such procedures may have decreased, risks do remain. Through prayer, ask God for wisdom and guidance, prior to proceeding with any *elective* permanent body modifications.

Thou Shall Not Expose Thy Undergarments In Public Areas

*Under*garments are to be worn *under* other clothing, as not to be seen. Unintentional exposure of undergarments signals that not enough time and attention has been allocated to ensure that outer garments are appropriate and have been paired with the correct undergarments. Take time to inspect and adjust your wardrobe accordingly. This is not a special request but a reasonable one, as told to us in Romans 12:1 ". . .present your bodies a living sacrifice, holy, acceptable unto God, *which is* your reasonable service."

Outer garments that are partially sheer should have a fabric lining in areas where undergarment exposure is at risk. Outer garments such as these may need to be paired with other outer garments to create a layering effect.

Make the choice to dismiss all fashion trends that deliberately call for undergarment exposure, this is not the fashion statement you want to make.

Often times these trends are started by those in the fashion design industry or the entertainment industry. These trendsetters may not have the Body of Christ in mind, when creating or perpetuating such fashion trends. Intentional undergarment exposure signals a lack of development and refinement of ones style maturity.

Just because a fashion trend becomes mainstream in our culture, does not mean it is appropriate for the Christian fashion maven. Be alert and pay attention to the design, cut and style of all garments. Christian appropriate garments, and Christian fashion styling will include an element of elegance and impeccable detailing.

Extra care must be given to ensure that Christian standards are met. "Let your light so shine before men, that they may see your good works, and glorify your Father which is in heaven" (Matthew 5:16).

Thou Shall Not Don Inappropriate Eye-Steering Apparel

Christian Accouterment For Women and inappropriate eye-steering apparel are mutually exclusive. Individuals will have differing opinions as to whether a particular garment or fashion accessory is appropriate or not. Allow the Holy Spirit to speak to you and closely monitor and adjust your wardrobe choices. Incline your ear and fine-tune your heavenly senses and God will speak to you to assist you with every wardrobe and fashion decision.

Posh Protocol™ reminds us that apparel that is designed to purposely accentuate female breasts, hips or buttocks in a sexually suggestive manner and steer your eye toward these areas is sending a message that is in contradiction to the message of the Gospel of Jesus Christ. Inappropriate eye-steering apparel may also contain symbols or wording to draw your attention to an area of the body in a sexually suggestive manner.

Investigate your motives and your message when choosing your wardrobe. Your wardrobe, your image and your presentation are speaking on your behalf before you ever say a word. Your non-verbal presentation *is* your introduction. What exactly are you saying, before saying anything? Does your non-verbal message appropriately represent your Christian walk? Or is your presentation making a self-disparaging remark or statement.

As a Christian woman, refuse to allow your personal presentation and wardrobe choices to be a distraction for someone who is seeking a relationship with God. As a representative of Christ, do not allow your behavior to be the reason someone rejects the message of the gospel and turns away from God. As a Christian Woman you have a responsibility to steer others toward Christ and not to steer them toward your physical attributes.

Thou Shall Not Don Accessories Bearing Ungodly Symbols or Insignia

In addition to apparel, ensuring accessories are the right fit, color, and style is another way in which we give honor unto God. Take a close look to ensure that every accessory that you own or plan to purchase, does not have any markings, symbols, shapes or wording that is dishonorable to God or perhaps even demonic. We would be remiss if we failed to evaluate our clothing accessories for appropriateness. Accessories include, hats, earrings, necklaces, rings, watches, scarves, belts, etc.

 Pay attention to writings or markings on these items and what they may symbolize. Human skulls or other death or demonic markings may be easy to spot or may be partially concealed within intricate design patterns. Yes, the details of your accessories do, in fact, matter. By donning accessories with ungodly symbols you may be unwittingly inviting in demonic spirits.

Accessories should also be complimentary to the garments you are wearing. Is the color or style appropriate for that particular garment? Is the statement the accessory is making too loud for the garment you are wearing? If you are wearing a beautiful garment, you do not want to wear an accessory that will draw too much attention away from the garment, thereby overshadowing the beauty of the garment.

Different occasions may call for jewelry and other accessories to be bold or reserved. There is a time for costume jewelry, fine jewelry and bespoke jewelry separately and perhaps all at the same time.

Review your entire collection of accessories frequently. Purge items from the collection and add to the collection when appropriate. Devise a sorting or organization system for these items. This will save time when choosing what to wear.

Thou Shall Not Don Pajamas Or Robes [Or Other Private Quarters Garments] In Public Areas

Resist the urge to just grab a jacket and wear your pajamas under it while you make a quick trip to the supermarket to pick up that one item that you absolutely need. Do not don bedroom loungewear and then venture out into public areas. While this may seem like a harmless gesture, it actually unveils a callous view toward Posh Protocol™. Pajamas, robes, fuzzy slippers are designed for use in private quarters. Take the few extra moments that are needed to find and put on clothing that is suitable for public viewing.

By wearing private quarters garments in public areas, you are allowing your audience to be privy to a part of you that is not meant for public viewing or public engagement. Respect your Father in heaven, whom you represent, and respect yourself enough to know how and when to differentiate between public and private garments.

Wearing private quarters garments in public areas creates a visual breach that allows trespassing into prohibited areas of ones life. The disrespect of oneself, silently gives permission to others to disrespect you as well. One way in which disrespect toward oneself occurs, is by failing to establish public and private personal appearance boundaries.

Please note, your audience is seated and engaged in focused observation *of you*. You are continually teaching others who you are and how to treat you with your behavior and non-verbal communication. Go to great-lengths to ensure that you are communicating a message of self-respect and Godly representation.

This commandment, as well as, all of the aforementioned commandments also applies to the person or persons in your charge, for which you will be making wardrobe decisions.

Thou Shall Not Omit [Full-Length Mirror] Wardrobe Checks

C.C. PRESTON ● DR. POSH ®

    Please perform wardrobe checks before going into public areas. These wardrobe checks are necessary to ensure that the style, fit and tailoring of garments are adequate. There are several Posh Protocol™ wardrobe checks that will allow you to determine if your final wardrobe selections are approved for wearing.

    Wardrobe Check I: Bow Down™. This wardrobe check requires you to bow down, bend forward at the waist approximately 45 degrees, as if in worship unto the Lord, and observe if any of your garments are gaping open or falling off the shoulder.

    Wardrobe Check II: Reach For Heaven™. This wardrobe check requires you to extend your arms upward reaching for heaven, as if in praise unto the Lord, and observe if any of your garments are gaping open, rising up, shifting or exposing your midriff.

Wardrobe Check III: Sit On The Alter™. This wardrobe check requires you to kneel down on both knees and lean forward approximately 45 degrees, as if in reverence unto the Lord on the alter, and observe if any of your garments are gaping open, drifting up or falling off the shoulder.

All observed, or potential, garment malfunctions should be evaluated to determine if the garment should be altered, covered with another garment or purged from your wardrobe. Before all public speaking appearances or events where you will be a featured guest, it is important that the garments you are planning to wear be even more closely critiqued. Standing on a podium under special lighting may change the appearance or opaqueness of garments. Prior to leaving your private quarters, perform a 360° hair, make-up, smile and wardrobe check, thrice, in front of a full-length mirror.

CONCLUSION

POSH PROTOCOL, Volume 1, The 10 Commandments of Christian Accouterment For Women, is Your Go-To Guide for how to personify Christ in everyday life with your personal appearance, manner of speaking and individual conduct.

We know that Posh Protocol™ is elegant etiquette in speech, adornment, actions or deeds and is thereby, a representation of the opulence of the Kingdom of God.

Each of the 10 Commandments, is a constructive tool to guide you into developing and refining your own personal representation of Christ. Your individual Posh Protocol™ will be speaking on your behalf before your audible voice is ever heard. Make sure your non-verbal message and your verbal message are a synchronous, eloquent testament of your love for God and his love for you. Don Your Diadem™ and take your rightful place in the Kingdom of God!

"...if thou shalt confess with thy mouth the Lord Jesus, and shalt believe in thine heart that God raised him from the dead, thou shalt be saved."

Romans 10:9

Prayer of Salvation

Heavenly Father, I confess I am a sinner. I repent of my sins. I believe your son Jesus Christ died for my sins. He was raised from the dead and He is alive right now. I accept Jesus Christ as my Lord and Savior now and forever. Lord, I surrender my life to you completely. Holy Spirit dwell within me and manifest your presence within me through an impartation of my own spoken heavenly language.
Amen

Disclaimer

While the author and publisher have used their best efforts in preparing this book, they make no representations with respect to the accuracy or completeness of the contents of this book and specifically disclaim any implied warranties.

The material contained herein is for general information purposes. The author, publisher and all affiliates accept no responsibility and exclude all liability in connection with the use or application of the information contained herein. Words or phrases followed by the trademark symbol (™) are the trademarked property of the author.

Dr. Posh® is the moniker given to C.C. Preston under the auspices of the Holy Spirit. The moniker Dr. Posh is connotative of her competence in the opulence of the Kingdom of God, Christian Protocol and Christian Etiquette and does not denote a doctoral or medical degree.

References

1. Posh. (n.d.). *Online Dictionary*. Retrieved April 7, 2017, from http://dictionary.com/browse/posh

2. Protocol. (n.d.). *Online Dictionary*. Retrieved April 7, 2017, from http://dictionary.com/browse/protocol

ABOUT THE AUTHOR

C.C. Preston, B.S., M.S., P.M.C., is **Dr. Posh® the Etiquettician®, The Protocol and Etiquette Specialist.**

C.C. Preston, Dr. Posh® is a woman after God's own heart. The Etiquettician®, Speaker and Consultant is also the Author of the Stiletto Etiquette Manifesto, STILETTO DOSSIER, which is a Godly instruction manual on how to personify the image of Christ while wearing Stilettos.

www.DrPosh.com

@IAmDrPosh / Social Media

P. O. S. H.
Prophesying Oracle Sent Here ™

www.ingramcontent.com/pod-product-compliance
Lightning Source LLC
LaVergne TN
LVHW051209080426
835512LV00019B/3179